Donut Famine

poems by
Rick Lupert

Baton Rouge New Orleans

Donut Famine
poems by
Rick Lupert

Copyright © 2016 by Rick Lupert
All rights reserved

Rothco Press

Design and Layout ~ Rick Lupert
Author Photo ~ Addie Lupert

This book is protected under the copyright laws of the United States of America. Any reproduction or other unauthorized use of the material or artwork herein is prohibited without the express written permission of the author except in the case of brief quotations embodied in critical articles and reviews.

First Edition ~ December, 2016

ISBN-13: 978-1-945436-11-6

Published by Rothco Press.
www.rothcopress.com

Visit the author online at
www.PoetrySuperHighway.com

My whole life, my whole soul, my whole spirit is to blow that horn.

- Louis Armstrong

[New Orleans is a city where one] can eat and drink the most and suffer the least.

- William Makepeace

If you're not having a good time in New Orleans you're entertainment handicapped.

- Dave, a New Orleans *Yat*

Thank you Addie, Greg, Mary, Bernie, Sara, Brendan, Elizabeth, Jonathan Penton, the concierege at the Roosevelt Hotel, the captive and free alligators in New York and Louisiana, the staff of First Class cabins everywhere, cavemen and cavewomen (their struggle was real), and the people of New Orleans who deserve only the very best.

To Addie who held my hand after every cocktail and made sure I didn't wander into the Mississippi River.

Prelogue
(a word I made up)

May, 2016

I tell Addie *in New Orleans*
you can pay to have an alligator
eat you.

We are a month away from
our trip and in, of all places,
Milwaukee.

She is not ready to
comment on this as we
walk up the Milwaukee River

looking for locally sourced
cheese. I tell her *this book*
isn't going to write itself.

She is not ready to
comment on that
either.

June 2016

My main goal for this trip is to not be eaten by an alligator.

Glad You're Here

You never want to arrive at the airport
so early the Starbucks isn't open yet.

The long line of pre five a.m. people
share a certain hopelessness and

inevitably you're at the end of that line
the most hopeless of all. Until

someone arrives later than you so
maybe they got a few minutes more sleep

but at the very least, due to their
position behind you, you have a certain

priority or higher ranking over them
which provides no comfort at all in this

miserable pre-coffee state of being.
I'm not even going to tell you what time

I woke up. Okay it was three a.m.
yes there's a three in the morning now too.

Welcome to vacation two thousand
and sixteen!

I Can't Find My Child in the Airport

Addie says he's right behind me
but no one has the energy to turn
around and verify this at three a.m.
even though it's five a.m. so I'm
just going to assume that is his
breathing and check closer when
we get to Syracuse in another
hundred years.

In The Airport Starbucks

I
I turn to Addie in the Starbucks line
which goes on for a hundred years
and ask her *do you think they have
coffee here?* Jude chimes in with
It's called Starbucks Coffee daddy!
That was for your mother to react to
I tell him and she points out that she
did slightly raise her eyebrow at the
query and that is all she is willing to
commit to at whatever time it is
in the morning.

II
I hold up the bag labeled *Gummy Pandas*
and Addie reacts with all the emotions there are.
All of them. (panda-monium)

III
We're all excited about the *Moon Cheese* snacks
though I think I'm going to hold out for
whatever they have edible from Jupiter.
(You can thank me now for not going with
the more obvious *Uranus*.)

IV
I've written so much about and in Starbucks
this morning I feel it necessary to point out
that they are not a sponsor of this book.
At least not yet.

The Dawn's Early Light

So many people I am related to are
saying things to me about airport
food and newly purchased sticker
books and it is too early in all the
time zones to process any of it.
I notice my fly is down which means
someone is falling down in the job.
I wonder if there's ever been a time
it was up. Certainly not this morning.
At least I think it is morning.
It is hard to tell without the
light the sun usually provides.

Impending Birthright

Obviously we are heading to New Orleans via Syracuse, New York. We'll be one child lighter for about a week. I've been listening to the local radio station to emotionally prepare myself. I wasn't born on the bayou but I suspect in ten days time I will claim to have been.

Your Big Fat Greek Father

You were just in Rochester and soon I'll be a spit away in Syracuse. How do we keep almost intersecting, thousands of miles away from where the Hollywood sign casts its shadow? I saw your father pretending to be Greek in a movie the other night which is easy for him since he is. I believed every word he said. Every eyebrow he lifted.

Flight Number One

I
A woman seated behind me accidentally
brushed my hair with her left knuckle.
She apologized, but sometimes that sliver of
human contact makes all the difference.

II
Everyone is in the best mood ever.
I wish there was a way to intonate
sarcasm in typing.

III
A flight attendant informs the first class cabin
she will not have time to serve a pre-departure
beverage. I don't know how those people
survive in those kind of conditions.

IV
Addie and I add our fingers to each other's phones.
Shared Touch ID is just one of the ways we
deeply intertwine.

V
We're in an airplane without TV monitors or
inflight wifi, which is, I assume, how
cavemen used to fly.

VI
I don't know how they settled on
thirty two thousand feet as the optimal
altitude for flying but I can't pee until we get there.
I can see the tops of mountains and science knows
more than I ever will.

VII
My wife the anarchist has gone off to pee
even thought the *Fasten Seatbelt* sign is
still on. I can see Las Vegas below and
what happens in the sky stays in the sky.

VIII
Thirty two thousand
feet and I can feel
every one of them.

PHL

I
The Philadelphia airport has a store called *Lick*.
Sadly, if you try to lick anything in the store
they ask you to leave.

II
Terminal F is the forgotten stepsister
of the Philadelphia airport terminals.

There's no people mover mechanically
transporting you to it from the other terminals.

This is what it must have been like
for caveman when they had to take the

long walk from terminal C
to Terminal F.

Flight Number Two

I
Our plane to Syracuse is so small
they hand each of us a wing when
we board.

II
There is tape holding pieces of
the inside of this plane together.
Generally speaking we feel that
is not a good sign.

III
Many flight attendants rush through
their rote memory of the safety
announcements. Not this one,
intonating every word with a
tangible purpose. By the time she
finishes, we're a already in Syracuse.

IV
A stranger takes an iPad Monopoly game
for the cause. The cause being our seven
year old sits next to the stranger while
his parents nap across the aisle.

V
Have you ever been to Syracuse
I ask Addie knowing full well she has

been to Syracuse several times and
furthermore, I have been with her

each time, so there's no way I don't
already know the answer to this

question, unless I have brain damage
or I'm not really me, and I AM really me.

So the raised eyebrow of non-response
in response to my question of whether

or not she has been to Syracuse is
well deserved and this small bug can't

figure out how to get out of the plane
window, and I'll tell you one thing for sure

I am not opening it for him, or her or
whatever other gender this small bug

may be.

VI
We're up near the Finger Lakes.
I wonder what other parts of the body
have lakes named after them.

VII
Our plane from Philadelphia is
heading straight back to Philadelphia.
Seems to me we could have saved
a lot of time if it just stayed there.

Syracuse and Environs

Low Flyer

My cousin Gregory noticed my fly was down
and doesn't say anything about it
until the next day. Figured it was just
a form of California welcome. I'm going
to have to double Addie's fly-watch salary
for the rest of this trip.

Parenting

We convince our son to go to the animal park in Chittenango by threatening to take play away for the rest of his life, or maybe it was the rest of the day. Whatever it was, he did agree to get in the car.

At the Chittenango Wild Animal Park

I
That's not good is what the
caretaker at the alligator show
says when the bigger alligator
takes the little one in its mouth
trying to get the tossed-in bacon.
Not good indeed my little
wild animal park.

II
I'd describe to you how far out
the reticulated giraffe stuck his
tongue to take a carrot from me,
but this is a family show.

III
A little girl wants to know
do you get giraffe slobber on you?
You do, but it's an extra three dollars.

IV
I ask the grizzly bear if
he shits in the woods.
He gives me a lengthy answer
which I did not understand
because I don't speak bear.

V
They don't start the shows on time here
which is either an affront or tribute to
nature considering how exact amount
of time it takes for the earth to revolve
around the sun (or so they tell me).

VI
I wonder if the Irish and the Amish
are related since they have the
same last syllable.

Holy crap the Jewish too!

VII
The Amish come to the zoo
on a school bus. All of them.
All the Amish are at the zoo
today. The non-horse powered
bus. All the Amish fit on
the one bus. They arrive too
late to see the smaller alligator
almost get eaten by the larger one
in a bacon induced rage.
Or the wild frog jump into
the alligator mouth, in an
unprecedented suicide that
will shatter the local frog
community. Let's have a
Jazz funeral.

We Visit My Mother at Poiley Tzedek Cemetery.

She's right where we left her a year ago, the winter
and the rains didn't quite do the job I thought they would.

Another man's gravestone is leaning up against my
grandmother's in a manner I can only guess my grandfather

wouldn't have approved of. We search for evidence of
their parents in this field of the dead that started with

the Scottish whose stones have yielded to the uncleared
weeds of spring. The Jews have made good use of

the lawnmowers of Syracuse and you can see evidence
of ancestors all the way up to where the top of the hill

meets the sky. Our son wanders into an Orthodox
family ceremony. Either an unveiling or *Yahrtzeit*.

He doesn't know, he just sees people and knows
he's one of them.

I see, in the Fayetteville Wegmans, a package of *finishing butter*.

My God I haven't even started yet.

The Flies Have No Lord

My cousin paces his house with a flyswatter
like an assassin. They suspect we brought
the flies with us from Los Angeles. I suspect
they followed. The evening involves much
fruitless, fly-less swatting.

Dictionation

Addie acknowledges she will wake me up at 4:30 in the morning with a word that doesn't sound like a word. She assures me no words will be spoken that early in the morning either. This, the language of the dark morning.

Louisiana Bound

Donut Famine

I
Dunkin' Donuts in the Syracuse airport
is out of donuts so I suggest they
change the name to just *Dunkin'* but
then I realize there's nothing to dunk.
So they might as well call it nothing,
just a silent gesture that no one
acknowledges, which seems much
nicer than my second idea which is
Fuck You I Want a Donut.

II
Addie thinks I'm making up the story
about the missing donut truck that the
woman at Dunkin' Donuts told me.

It's not exactly that they're out of donuts.
The donuts never arrived. They called and
called the donut truck and no-one answered.

Sadly it's all true (unless the donut lady
was lying to me) and now Addie is concerned
there's been an accident and there's a truck

with donuts hanging out somewhere
on the thruways of the great state
of New York.

Flight Number Three

I
We're lucky enough to be flying First Class
and I smile at all the steerage passengers
as they take their long walks to their seats
because I want them to know I'm still one
of them, as I sip my donut-less coffee in my
extra wide seat, with leg room cavemen
never dreamed of.

II
A bumblebee in the plane has really taken
to the First Class businessman across the aisle
from us. I think it flies down his shirt and he flails
more wildly than a businessman should and I'm
tired of these mother fleepin' bumblebees on this
mother fleepin' plane.

III
I assume the coach class passengers only get
common house flies instead of bumblebees.

IV
I assume the professional voice over with flight
safety announcements can only be heard by us
while the coach class passengers get their
information delivered in cockney accents by
the unkempt cast of Off-Broadway *Oliver*.

V
The house flies at Greg and Mary's
The bumblebee in first class* —
We are bringing the apocalypse
with us wherever we go.

*I don't mean to ruin it for you but
it turns out it was just a beetle.

VI
I think Vin Diesel is our flight attendant
or somewhere between Vin Diesel and
The Rock, or I'm tired of these mother
fruitloopin' actor flight attendants on
this mother fruitloopin' plane.

VII
I tell Addie something that is not true
about Leprechauns servicing First Class
passengers in some way and she reminds
me we are not going to Ireland, so I change
it to the French aristocracy which is
pointless as she stopped believing me
about four books ago.

Glancing at the cover of this book will make this poem unnecessary.

This early in the trip I don't know what this book will be called. But I assure you, it will be called something.

PHL Again

There's a wasp on the shuttle between
terminals F and A at the Philadelphia
airport. The insects we encounter are
getting more and more dangerous
with each form of transportation we take.
I expect our rental car in Louisiana
will come with an entire hive
of man eating alligator hornets.

Trust

The first thing I'm going to do
when we get to Louisiana
is exchange all my money
for Cajun voodoo currency
with the first reputable
looking guy I see who seems
at all interested in my wallet

Flight Number Four

I
Flying first class to New Orleans –
I could get used to this.
Both the first class part
and the to New Orleans part.

II
We land at Louis Armstrong's airport.
If I walk off this plan and am not
showered with satchmo, I'm
getting right back on.

III
Judd
the flight attendant

gives me a bottle of
red wine and says

enjoy New Orleans.
I think we're all in love.

Ready to go wild in NOLA

a sign at the airport asks.
Not just yet NOLA. Gonna
get a toot frisky in Baton Rouge.
Ask me again on Friday.

An Afternoon and Evening in Baton Rouge

At the Old Governor's Mansion

I
It was only *old* because they built
a newer one which, by today's standards
is also old.

II
Huey Long wanted to be president
so he built the governors mansion like
the White House. It even has a small oval
office for when small presidents come along.

III
Bradley the guide, a French Cajun, has the
accent of his ancestors. Pronounces "venue"
ven-you. Like it's French of something.

IV
Huey was assassinated in his forties
Bradley tells us. *Weren't we all* I tell him.

V
Straw hats in the summer,
felt in the fall was the fashion
of the day, Bradley tells us,
depending on which day
it was.

V
We see the first governor
who went to jail. He
was not the last

VI
Every Man a King, and
My First Days in the White House
were the books Huey Long wrote.
Have you read them?

VII
Bradley sends us up the secret stairs
by ourselves. Says he'll meet us in the
master bedroom. I don't think he wants
his spouse to know. I don't see a ring
on his finger, but I bet he just keeps it
common law.

What's Going On With My Finger?

Addie wants to know what's going on with my finger as it fails again to activate the camera on my phone. *What's going on with your finger* she asks me. As if that's a question that wouldn't be written down.

At the Hilton

I
The sassy elevator voice lady is here.
She says *eighth floor* the way we want her to.
Then *going down* with the tired Eeyore-like
depression we find comforting.

II
Our hotel has "non irritating"
mouth wash in the bathroom.
I'm not sure why they would
make any other kind.

Two Thoughts on Water

I
I tell Addie we could
float down the Mississippi River
from Baton Rouge to New Orleans
when we're done here.

I think it's a good idea and
we could save a day on the rental car.
Addie is shaking her head the whole time.

II
I ask Addie
if you jump up when it's raining
if you're technically swimming.
She is still shaking her head.

Context

Addie wants me to note
that the previous poem
was written after my first
cocktail in Louisiana.

Two More Thoughts on Water

I
The water in Baton Rouge is hard.
How hard? Calculus. That's pretty hard.
I know.

II
I'm pretty sure I'm going
to throw my phone into the
Mississippi River.

Coast to Coast

There are slim pickings in Baton Rouge
in terms of food we are willing to put
in our mouths and consequently
we are focusing on the buildings we
can go inside and the things they tell us
in there, and the extraordinary southern
hospitality and the mighty Mississippi River
hidden behind the blackout curtains in our
hotel room. We'll see her tomorrow. And
everyday until this is all over and we fly to
every other coast this fine nation
offers to humanity.

Barely Coherent

I'm falling asleep while writing.
Too many time zones in too few days.
Please tell me what you read here.
I don't want to miss a thing.

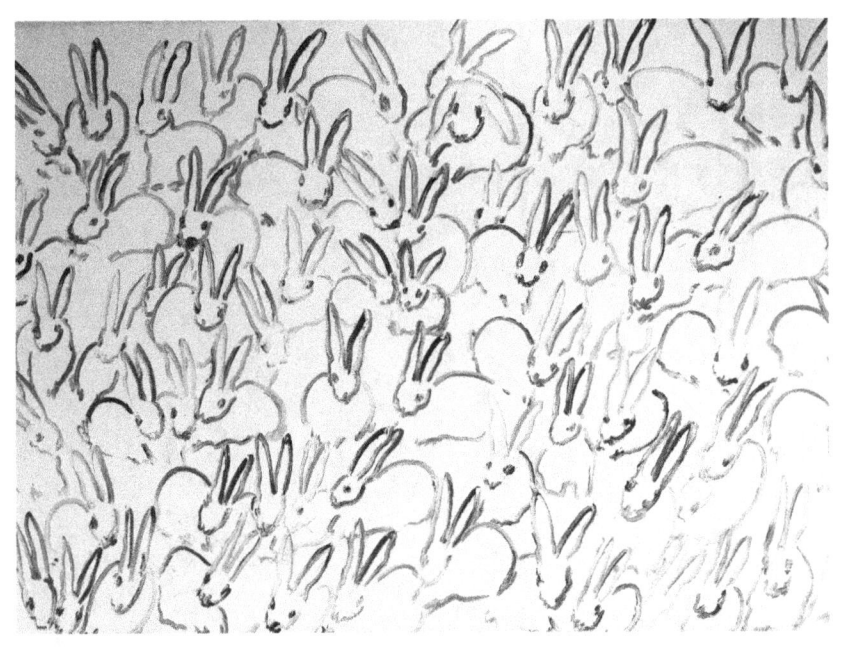

A Full Day in Baton Rouge

At the Red Stick Farmers Market

I
I ask the lawyer standing at the counter
at our breakfast place if I can sue them
for not having the potatoes which were
listed on their website. He says yes and
we all have a good laugh but then he
secretly slips me his card...

II
It wasn't easy to choose between the
table with the painting of the watermelon,

the one with the strawberries, or the one
with the sunflowers.

Ultimately we went with the strawberries
for mundane reasons I won't bore you with.

(Though send me an email if you'd
really like to know.)

III
Addie was happy enough with
her crepe style omelet this morning

though it didn't come with the potatoes
the website promised so she's not as

full as she could be which leads to the
declaration that she *might be sucking*

on a packet of peanut butter later on.
Oh Addie, the Louisiana State Museum

couldn't be more excited for your arrival.
We finish our coffee forged out of the

Mississippi River, walk away from tables
whose tops are painted with strawberries,

watermelon and sunflowers (how did they
know we'd be here) and walk north on

Fifth Street to learn everything about
the capitol of this river-born state.

At Capitol Park Museum

I
Thomas Jefferson arranged the purchase
of Louisiana for fifteen million dollars.
These days you can't even buy a private island
for that amount of money.

II
Thanks to our recently acquired knowledge
we are able to answer the surprise quiz
in The Capitol Park museum about what
the Louisiana state bird is. It's the brown pelican.
And now I have passed this knowledge on
in case another such a quiz surprises you.

III
The last battle of the War of 1812
or the *second American Revolution*
was fought and won in Louisiana.
Now we're all great friends.

IV
A waitress a long time ago
said *anyone who says anything
not nice about Huey Long
is a big meany.*

And the biggest meany of all is
the one who assassinated him
in 1935.

Louis Armstrong at the Capitol Park Museum

I
Just want to say that music has no age.
As long as you are still doing something
interesting and good. You are in business
as long as you are breathing.
Yeah.

II
My whole life,
my whole soul,
my whole spirit is
to blow that horn.

III
Armstrong claimed he was born
on July 4, 1900 which was a genius idea
in terms of needing to do quick math to
determine how old you were.

IV
A note is a note
in any language.

Back at the Capitol Park Museum (Not that we left)

I
Much of Louisiana was created by sediment
from the changing course of the Mississippi River.
Its current course was established in 999 AD
which has me wondering what it has planned next.

II
Floods keep clearing the poor people
out of southern Louisiana, partially because
of the water, but also because of the wealthier
people who push them to the back of the relief lines.

When the Water Comes

        When the water comes

we'll be wearing capris.
We'll need to get the canoe
out from behind the door
at the art gallery.
We'll take it seriously.

        When the water comes

the man in the next room
will be quiet.
The shampoo will be where
it's supposed to be.
The loose clothing we wear
to tolerate this weather
won't help.

        When the water comes

people will finally
update their websites.
Museums will stay open at night.
The railroad track won't
frighten us.

> When the water comes

you'll get a silk tie with any
animal you want on it.
The second line parades
will happen year-round.
Your neck pain will disappear.

> When the water comes

by definition the drought
will be over.
Your accent will not define you.
You will go to sleep, and
when you wake up, it
will still be there.

We are Still at the Capitol Park Museum

I
Some land owners put up signs that said
"Landowner in support of black bear restoration."
I want to put up a sign that says "Poet in support
of land owners who support black bear restoration."

II
I'm not sure why president Theodore Roosevelt
felt the need to hunt for a trophy Louisiana Black Bear.
All I can tell you is I didn't vote for him.

III
I take hold of a steamboat steering wheel
and pilot this museum all the way to Canada.

IV
That toilet in the Capitol Park Museum
flushes before I am done with it,
taking all of my dignity with it.

V
They're still debating the definitions of
and distinctions between Cajun and Creole
so don't expect me, a boy from the
San Fernando Valley via central New York
(not to mention Plantation, Florida and
Englewood, New Jersey)
to clear it up here.

VI
It turns out Elvis really did leave a building
and that's why we say that.

(It was the Shreveport YMCA in 1956.)
These days when I leave a building,

well nothing really.

VII
The exact origins
of Mardi Gras are
unknown, but about
thirty seconds into it
nobody cares.

VIII
Balls were first held
in the eighteenth century
though I suspect that was
going on much earlier.

Only One Observation at the New State Capitol Building Where the Elevators Were Broken So We Couldn't Go Up to the Observation Deck

The governor has
his own elevator in
the new state capitol
building. Solid gold
doors. A man of the
people. The golden
people.

(It's possible it's a woman.)

The dress code at City Bar on Third Street north of Florida Street

has more items on it than I had the tolerance to count and includes the phrase "no underwear tolerance." I get the feeling it would be easier to walk in there naked than worry what shade of white my sneakers are.

Red Stick Pride

Much of the exhibitry in Baton Rouge references New Orleans, as if this city doesn't deserve its own identity.

In the Old State Capitol

Every man a king, but no one wears a crown.
Huey Long, Campaign Slogan, 1928

I
We learn strawberries are the state fruit.
That's the only thing we learn in the room which,
on the map we're told, we would learn all about
the assassination of Huey Long. Perhaps he
was killed by a strawberry.

(Later we realize we were looking at the wrong
floor on the map. But we do find out that they're
not a hundred percent sure who killed him, so
it hasn't been disproven that it was a strawberry.)

II
Baton Rouge
means *red stick*.
I wonder if they
have one in
the gift shop.

III
When I get home
I'm leading the effort
to rename Van Nuys
Van Nuys Parish.

IV
The Old State Capitol building
was restored six times in
1938, 1946, 1956, 1966
1986, and 1993. I know
a detail oriented contractor
in Van Nuys who could have
done the job right the first time.

Red Stick

*If you're going to name your city 'Red Stick'
you could at least have the courtesy to have
one sticking up out of the ground that we can
look at* is what I would say if I didn't just learn
there is such a stick at the original settlers point
which is a little too far out of downtown for
us to have had the courtesy to visit it.

Wet Semantics

I ask Addie, next to a fountain which shoots water out of the ground as kids jump through the jets,

if you jump in water that shoots out of the ground are you technically swimming?

Addie is not ready to expand her definition of swimming at all yet.

At LSU Museum of Art

I
Crouching Boy in Deerskin Camouflage
Ying Dynasty 13th-14th century

One of the earliest examples of
S & M culture in Chinese culture.

II
The wall of bunnies by Hunt Slonem
in the Louisiana State University Art Museum
at the Shaw Center on the fifth floor
is something everyone should see.

III
The wall of Creole Uniplat spoons (1739)
makes me want to nail my spoons
to the wall back home (2016).

IV
I don't really have anything interesting
to say about the lenticular prints except
now I know that's what they are called.

V
Wonder Woman
Nicole Charbonnet, 2010

Addie says this would make
a cool t-shirt but I'm only
willing to make it happen if
Wonder Woman is willing
to wear a t-shirt with
Addie on it.

VI
Caught II
Elizabeth Shannon, 1989

An alligator climbing up a ladder
on the wall – I wonder if this is one
of those things like the eye glasses
someone left on the floor of a museum
that people gathered around and photographed.
Maybe this alligator walked up these ladders
froze there and they put up a descriptive card.

VII
Addie offers to become a sculpture
after we arrive at the rooftop sculpture garden
only to find no sculptures at all. I tell her to go
for it but in the end she declines.

VIII
We're in Baton Rouge too early to enjoy
Cow Appreciation Day according to a
calendar we see in the museum lobby.

IX
Lu Lu Takes a Dip
Denise Greenwood-Loveless, 2016

I guess that means she went swimming
regardless of what anyone says.

X
It occurs to me the artist's name
might be Denise Greenwood and
the artwork called *Loveless Lu Lu
Takes a Dip*. I hope they both find
love either way.

The Casino Only Gets One Poem

Seven people enter the elevator at
the Hollywood Riverboat Casino

past a sign that clearly says "Six
People Maximum. Overloading will

lead to equipment failure and entrapment."
One woman is very nervous about this.

Another says "it won't get stuck."
I tell the assembled group of Acadians

I can't think of any other group of
people I'd rather be stuck in an elevator

with. Building community one group of
people in an elevator at a time.

Thomas	Billy Lorimer	Charlotte	Pallas
Onufre	Henriette	Justine	Do
Alfred	Thomas	Rosetta	Eugene
Maurice	Servilie	Susan	Paris
Andre	Trosine	Benoit	Jenny
Rose	Soulougue	Prince	Mars
Moses	Mercury	Francoise	Nancy
Felonise	Adele	Albert	Paul
Michel	Benedict	Ida	Louis
Julia	Felicite	Codjo	Martin
Toni	Marie Angelina	Louise	Jules
Ursule	Grand Joseph	Tom	Adam
Elise	Roselia	Raymond Ox	Bazile
Flore	Euphrosine	Theotis	Gognon

We Leave Baton Rouge We Visit Plantations We Arrive in New Orleans

Premonition

White shirt
Black coffee

Later green
mint julep

Disaster's comin'
to the bayou

Battle of the Mug Lickers

While reminding me the
mint juleps at the plantation
might not contain alcohol
I lick my coffee mug at Addie.
She stops talking and licks hers
and says "I'll see your lick."
The game begins...

Addie Thoroughly Enjoys Her Paleo Scone

*I'd like to paleo your goods
like I did last night, remember?*

Yes, I remember, she says which
is a much less dismissive response

than the one she gave me in Paris
twelve years ago when she was hungry.

Bathroom Signs are Getting Too Vague

The bathroom at Magpie cafe has a bottle of milk with an M on it.

Either this is for me, or this is where dairy products go to ferment.

P.S. The one on the women's bathroom has an F on it which I'm sure stands for *Filk*.

I don't see a single Starbucks in Baton Rouge

Come to think of it I don't see a married one either.

Driving the 10 East to New Orleans

or actually to the Laura Plantation,
where, if all goes as planned our tour

will not be in French. I tell Addie we
could take this road all the way to Florida,

or back home. But we'd have to turn around,
if we wanted to do that. I'm not sure if I want

her to be impressed by my knowledge of this
road, or feel the same nostalgia I feel on this

segment of highway that I've never been on.
I wonder if they could ship Jude back to L.A.,

I continue, to break the tension – *and by L.A.
I mean Los Angeles,* and not Louisiana, which

is something you have to specify in this neck
of the bayou.

I'm Excited to Go to New Orleans

No offense Baton Rouge, but you change
your restaurant menus without telling anyone.

You can't tell that you're on a river boat when
you step on to your river boat casinos. Why

else would you go on a river boat casino?
You have a rich history but in every sentence

you mention New Orleans. Do you think they
talk so much about you? I'm exited for

New Orleans too, Baton Rouge. Your red stick,
where is your red stick?

A billboard tells me

You will meet God when you die
but it doesn't specify when that will be.
You can't count on billboards to get all
the information you need.

Listen to this

http://bit.ly/2b75K6H

At Laura Plantation

I
The guide cautions us to
not lean up against the brick walls
under the house or else we'll be
orange for the rest of the day
which no sensible people want
in today's political climate.

II
I sit in a rocking chair on the
porch of the Laura Plantation
in the humidity awaiting a Mint Julep
that will last for the rest of my days.

III
The most important thing Flagy Duparc
did for the family was die. The seven
million dollars in silver and gold coins
he left made quite an impact

IV
Laura Locoul lived
from Lincoln to Kennedy
From the Civil War to civil rights

V
A picture of Laura with a cardinal
(not the bird) on her one hundredth
birthday congratulating her on her
lifelong Catholicism sits next to one
of her dressed as Mephistopheles.

VI
I like the details in the doors
in the plantation's house and
besides taking a picture I decide
to save time by calling them *doortails*.

VII
We hear screaming and are relieved
to learn it's just a goat until our guide
tells us they're getting it ready for supper
which we don't find at all comforting.

VIII
The Duparc family owned
one hundred and ninety
human beings in 1850
as if such a thing was possible.

IX
Descendants of these slaves
lived in these cabins through
the 1970s.

X
The Laura Plantation is well maintained
today by people who make a decent living
wage to do so.

XI
The instructions on how to properly use
the bathroom at the Laura Plantation are
almost as long as the dress code list at
City Bar in Baton Rouge. Sorry. Did you not
want our experience at Laura to end with
a bathroom image? Let's just say the
plantation's cat is named Marianne (say it
in French) and she is the queen.

XII
The humidity while touring these plantations –
I hope all of New Orleans is indoors.

At Oak Alley Plantation

I
I'm sipping a mint julep on the porch of
the Oak Alley Plantation. A sign nearby
says *don't ring the bell*. I want to ring
the bell so bad it hurts my soul.

II
The word *famous* next to Oak Alley Mint Juleps
that come out of their mint julep machine is
probably famous as in everyone has heard of
the plague as well.

III
Cows broke into the house and lived here
for five years ruining the marble floors.

IV
Every time we enter an ornate restored dining room
I tell Addie in my fancy accent *we will dine here tonight*.
She's getting the guest list ready.

V
The French don't eat to live.
They live to eat.

VI
We're told the average French creole was
under five feet tall. I love them and their
giant expensive spoons.

VII
The shoo-fly fan in the dining room,
they think, is original to the house.
They found it in the attic and it
was operated by a slave boy.

VIII
I have determined, by my incoming
case of the vapors, that there is
real bourbon in this mint julep

IX
The rolling pin in the funeral room
may not be a rolling pin at all.

X
There's a pineapple
on the master bedroom bed.

They say if a bed had two pineapples
on it in the morning it meant the guests
had overstayed their welcome.

I'm only going to communicate in
multiples of pineapples from now on.

XI
Interview With a Vampire was filmed here.
So now it's a goth-emo mecca

XII
We arrive at Sugarcane Theater where
the video will begin in two and a half minutes
which is exactly the amount of time we need to
do what we need to do.

XIII
The Sugarcane Theater video tells us
everything we know to be unhealthy about sugar
is a myth.

It doesn't cause diabetes or anything bad.
Addie wants the next film shown to be the
documentary called *Sugar Blues*

which has factological information that
disputes everything we just saw. Though it does
end with a nice sugar-based folk song.

XIV
I'm not sure if it's just in my nature to start
singing along with the sugar cane song
or if that's just the mint julep singing.

XV
I observe that the slave laundry kettles
and the sugar kettles looked similar
which Addie agrees to as it says that
on the sign she just read.

XVI
Sick house Doctor Merriq believed
it was easier to amputate than repair.
He would bury the amputated pieces
believing they'd be reunited with their
owner in the next life.

XVII
In the restaurant, at the next table, a couple
is greeted by the manager and handed a flash drive
as they discuss *the piece* the woman is working on.
They wonder about high resolution pictures
and I hear the word *Dropbox* said with a southern
accent. *Flash drive, Dropbox* — terms the slaves and
even the rich plantation owners of this land
never dreamed of. Now the chef has come
I wonder what technologies he will add to the fray.

XVIII
My wife's new angle is forty-five.
When I tell her this, she responds with
a number of other angles, one of which
I would describe as *the pigeon*.

XIX
We learn in the gift shop that *Madame X*,
John Singer Sargent's famous painting,
which now hangs in the Met in New York City,
was a woman from New Orleans who was
famous for being allegedly *infidelicious* in
Paris which is a lot of cities and information
and a made up word all for one painting.

XX
Oh here we go I say
pointing to the a wooden B
in the gift shop. Well get this for
our son Bude. Addie's head shake
reminds me his name is not Bude.

XXI
A sign in the gift shop asks us
if we think the pecan is just
another nut. *Oh anything but
Mister pecan caricature.
Anything but.*

XXII
Hoes cause permanent damage
from consistent overuse according
to a sign in the slave exhibit and
anyone's common sense.

XXIII
Two hundred and three slave's names
are engraved on the wall of a cabin.

Two hundred and three people's names
are engraved on the wall of a cabin.

All that is left of them.

XXIV
Men are the sub
Women a sliver of the moon

according to outhouse
gender carving designations.

The women I know are
complete bodies rivaling

everything that floats
in the sky.

XXV
Using the bathroom at the magnificent
Oak Alley Plantation –

Our crops are saved!

New Orleans Day One

We enter New Orleans

a city that shouldn't exist. With this water table you might as well build on the floor of the Gulf. We enter New Orleans. *This city will never die.*

Uber

I
Our driver tells us the pumping stations
keep New Orleans from reverting
into a swamp. We humans and our
shenanigans against nature.

II
We drive by a jail and a sign says
don't pick up strangers. Okay sign
we won't.

The driver tells us the building with
no windows is the administration
and the one with windows is where
the prisoners are. Rehabilitation begins
with architecture.

III
A billboard tells us to *Get Kinky.*
Our driver would prefer we not.

Horns and Drums

I
The second line has
come to Bourbon Street

and I'm ready to show
everyone my tits.

The streets are running hot
and cold with liquor.

I have never felt more like
I was in a place than now.

II
Two cowbells and
the cheeks of the middle guy

are what Addie remembers
about the band that launched us

into Bourbon Street. One cowbell
is never enough.

In the Rue Royal Art Gallery

A couple are taken into a private room
for a properly lit viewing of the
twenty four thousand dollar *Hulk* piece.

We think the smaller one of
the rear view of the scantily clad
woman would go good in Jude's

room because of his affinity for
naked butts. Addie prefers the one
with the more subtle butt.

Bourbon Street

The man holding the *Two For One* sign is standing right next to the woman with the *Three For One* sign. We're hoping a battle to the death breaks out or in the spirit of New Orleans they combine their forces and offer a *Five For Two* special.

No Titties, No Beads

Beads raining out of the sky.
It seems magical until one guy
yells *No titties, no beads!*
Then the magic changes
just a little.

Sazarac

I order a Sazerac
In The Sazerac.
It's my first time
having one and my
first cocktail in New Orleans.
So don't skimp on the perfect
I tell the waitress who laughs
and hopefully takes me as
seriously as I need to be taken.

haiku

Those horns and drums. Those
horns and drums. Those horns and drums.
Those horns and drums. Those

The Bathroom Remodel Continues

I'm buying cabinets in Van Nuys
from a bed in New Orleans.
What a world.

Not to Get Eaten by an Alligator

The alligators are circling the
Roosevelt Hotel. They've heard
we're all sleeping and figure
this is the best time to make
their move. Major flaw in their
plan – They forgot to take door
opening lessons. They flap
their mouths open and close
hoping the sight of their teeth
will move us to surrender
like that frog in Syracuse
who jumped right into an
open mouth.

Lights Out New Orleans

at least in this room where
the beads hang over the
chaise lounge. The ice
melts in the container
especially designed for
ice. The hands pine
to be wrapped in
devices that will
hold them stationary.
Where the
lines get
shorter.
The eyes
get more
closed.

New Orleans Day Two or Our First Full Day in New Orlenas

The Roosevelt Hotel

I
This hotel is luxurious
but we do miss the
talking elevator lady
of yesterday.

II
There're some mighty fine toasters
in Teddy's Cafe at the Roosevelt.
The kind you'd bring home to momma.

Bourbon Street at Nine A.M.

is not Bourbon Street.
A hosed down daytime
tourist purgatory
Cars can drive in the
street for Godsake!
Only one guy with a beer
for miles. The remnants
of voodoo nights washed
into the drains.

They Knew I Was Going to Write This

St. Peter Street by Jackson Square
is medium lane. Medium, as in psychic.
A certain subset of people knew that
without me telling them.

Cafe du Monde

I'd like to describe the experience
of beignets and chicory coffee at
Cafe du Monde.

Our waitress is a hundred years old
and the queen of Asia. I see a man
open his mouth wide to take a beignet

in there, leaving residue of powdered
sugar when he's done. Our beignets come
and I become the man

whose face is covered with sugar while
people less experienced than I look on.
Look, there's a baby

having his first beignet.
Or maybe it's hers. Who
can tell these days?

On the French Quarter Walking Tour

I
Our German tour guide
uses the word *Kosher*
in the spirit of the creole
mixing of cultures.

II
We see beignets being made.
Dough cut, then tossed
backwards without looking.
Without fail they land in the oil.
The people are fed.

III
Even Darth Vader is
busking in the French Quarter.

He dances to
The Imperial March

while our guide tells us about
the black code.

I shout to him
Long live the rebellion!

Not the recruitment
result he had hoped for.

IV
Baldwin Wood's Pumps
haven't stopped working
since they were made
in 1912. He was the world's
expert on pumping cities dry,
so we're told.

V
Thanks to the *Code Noir*
slaves could purchase
their own freedom. As if
such a thing was possible.

VI
Article number one of the Code Noir
says Jews are not allowed.

VII
We walk by a sign that says the Pimm's Cup
was the original New Orleans cocktail.
I want to argue with the sign since I know
it was the Sazarac but I'm going to wait
until the sign becomes sentient so it
will be a two way exchange of ideas.

VIII
An Ursuline nun wrote to her father
in France that the Aristocratic women
in New Orleans were ignorant but
excellent at displaying their beauty.

IX
For years of successful praying
the Ursuline nuns were allowed
to ride the street cars for free, until
the mid nineteen eighties. No one
is sure what they did to lose that privilege.
At least no one on this tour.

X
We stop by the birthplace of
Danny Barker who brought the banjo
and revitalized the brass band tradition
and trained the Marsalis brothers.
I'd like to emphasize he was a
jazz banjoist.

XI
Don't be in a hurry in New Orleans.
You'll just get sweaty. Our guide tells
us in front of an old spaghetti factory.
Not the chain restaurant but a building
where they actually made spaghetti.
(in case you were wondering why I
didn't capitalize "old spaghetti factory.")
Her friend Betsy walks by.

XII
Everything that touches air
has to be approved by the
Vieux Carre Commission.
I'm touching air. I'm not sure
why I get a free pass.

XIII
I get a little scared when
the tour guide, on what turned out
to be a private tour of the French Quarter
tells us *I can go all day!* It's impressive.
But as close as possible to the
allotted two hours please.

XIV
We're so hungry after the tour
we skip the second line parade
that breaks out to go directly
to the restaurant. I hope to God
another one comes along before
we have to go. Otherwise this
hunger will have been my most
grave mistake.

Wishful Reading

I misread a sign and think it says
The Boobs Museum.

I'd like to see their exhboobits.
(Boobxhibits?)

I wonder if they have any special
exhibtits?

At the Presbytère

I
It is common for New Orleans residents
to keep an axe in their attic to use in case
a flood forces them into it and they need
to hack through the roof.

II
A man builds a cage to rescue his seven cats.
Conditions force him to leave them behind.
He left food and water and access to the roof.
When he returns weeks later, four of the cats
are still there. Three are gone.

The 1850 House

*This is where we will dine tonight
I tell Addie in my fancy voice in the
dining room of the 1850 House.
Peasants! Remove the chicken and
bring in a toficken,* I continue.

Wealth Planning

All these people who paint themselves
gold or white or bronze and pose as statues
until people give them money makes me think
one can of paint and I could be a millionare.

We Should Be Dancing

I do my jig of long pants falling
all the way to my ankles and ask
Addie to join in. She shows me just
pulling the cuffs down to her ankles
and asks me to join in. I'm a little
surprised she's not more excited
about the jig.

Jumpsuit Nightmare

Addie sees a lot of people in jumpsuits and explains she wouldn't want to wear one because, first of all it would be a nightmare to pee. A reasonable enough statement but the way she says it, I'm picturing something out of a Tim Burton movie – lightning, macabre music and everything just a little dark and exaggerated. She'll have to approve this poem so if you're reading it, you know what happened.

New Orleans is a Divided City

Mainly by streets. Though you
can walk from neighborhood to
neighborhood and no one will
tell you a thing. I'll take a cue
from the restroom sign at Carmo
on Julia Street which says
Restroom For Humans which
I believe apples to everyone.

Inclusivity

The sign said *Restroom for Humans*.
I saw several disappointed American
bison walk by.

Hurricane

Standing in line at Preservation Hall
on St. Peter Street. I've already thrown
away the Hurricane from two doors down.
They invented it there so it's probably
the best one you can get. After just
a handful of sips, it'll probably be my
last. The plastic cup thrown away
in the trash can in front of Pat O'Briens.
It's famous so my dissension will have
little effect. It's not my intention to have
any effect. I just want to hear the Jazz
All Stars. A collective of New Orleans
musicians who keep this place afloat.
That's the issue with New Orleans,
trying to stay afloat. It's not just the
water from the river. It's the humidity
pouring water off all the people.
I can hear their second to last set
through the wall. We're in for the third
and last. There will be no hurry. Despite
my wife's tired eyes and twenty thousand
steps. This night could go on all night.

It's Happening People!

A giant lizard person walks down the street and touches everyone. No, it's not the few sips of Hurricane. This is New Orleans! This is what happens here. The Lizard person wants tips. If I was a giant Lizard person, I would be a millionaire.

Jazz Wind

The way those Preservation Hall boys
Blow wind out of their mouths

They've got the cheeks of a hundred men.
The Jazz cat Sweets in the entry way

is as cool as   a cat. He won't complain
if you pet him, but he's not going to

let you know how much he likes it either.
I'm going to feel this wind on the other

side of the Mississippi, on the other side
of the Rockies, on the other side of the desert

all the way to the Pacific where the orange trees
fight off the ocean. Jazz. New Orleans.

Away with me.

New Orleans Day Three

The Creator Cured Child Uber Driver

This may be the last time we see our Uber driver Reggie. He's about to be a multi-millionaire with an invention I can't tell you about. He's the baby with no throat. The miracle child Uber driver, all grown up and about to change the world. www.thecreatorcuredchild.org

The poetry section at the Garden District Book Shop

is one book by Kahlil Gibran.
But who am I to define what poetry is?
It could also be every other book in the store,
including the extensive Anne Rice section.
She lives in the neighborhood so probably
keeps the stock up herself.

Things We See and Learn On the Garden District Walking Tour

I
Canal Street divided the city
The French street names on that
side, are different from the English
ones on this side.

II
Our tour guide Dave is
a *Yat*. As in a guy who says
Where y'at?

III
*If you're not having
a good time in New Orleans
You're entertainment
handicapped.*

IV
In the Lafayette Cemetery
there are multiple people per tomb.
When they need more room, they
take the remains out of the oldest coffin
and put them in the compost pit at
the bottom.

V
According to markings on one family tomb
Guido Korndorffer had the incredible fortune
of being named after his ancestor
Guido Korndorffer.

VI
We hear a horn outside of the cemetery.
Just a solo player, no Jazz funeral.
But the day is young.

VII
James Hagan the tomb builder
built his own tomb and it looks
pretty cool.

VIII
According to Dave
more words were written
in New Orleans
but fewer read.

IX
Dave tells us the hardest restaurant
to get into is the Hard Rock Cafe.
Everyone with any reasonable
sensibility of New Orleans food culture
faints upon hearing this information.

X
Every guide and driver mentions
the crape myrtle trees so I thought
I'd mention them too.

XI
Dave tells us windows that go
all the way to the floor are called
guillotine windows.

XII
Dave tells us about the petticoat staircase
with two sets of steps ascending to the same
entryway so gentlemen could go up separately
and not see the ankles of their lady counterparts.

XIII
Bryan Bell who has a website called
Lessons in Lifemanship has a plaque
outside his house which says
On this site in 1897 nothing happened.
One has to admire his attention
to historical detail.

XIV
If this house isn't haunted
I'll mail my left foot to the
Voodoo queen.

XV
Some free people of color
owned slaves. Sometimes it
was there own family. As if
such a thing was possible.

XVI
Forget *melting pot*.
New Orleans is the
gumbo of the nation.

XVII
The Saints logo adorns
everything here including
the trash cans. Even the
garbage is holy.

XVIII
I don't mean to pressure myself
or my child, or anyone's child but
Trombone Shorty started playing
at four years old.

XIX
This three hundred year old tree
predates all the nonsense.

XX
Colonel Short's villa has been
for sale for a year and a half now.
I wish I was tall enough to buy it.

XXI
The famous people's homes
in the Garden District are not
hidden away behind forests,
impenetrable walls or gates.
You can ring the doorbell of
John Goodman if you have
good reason to do so.

Marketing

Any sandwich on French Bread is a PoBoy
we over hear a native in a coffee shop say
so I guess I have had one before.

Get Ready to Laugh Heartily

Our Uber driver asks
how it is in the cemetery.
*Not a lot of movement from
the residents* I tell her
once again displaying
the universality of my
world class wit.

Preparing for War

Addie is ready for a nap en route to the National WWII Museum. *Perhaps there will be a nap exhibit* I suggest hopefully.

At the National WWII Museum

I
Mike Mervosh was
trained in misery

because battle was full of it.
He was one of thirty one survivors

of his three hundred fifty one member troop.
Thank you Mike for what

you did there and for enduring
the things you saw

II
War is not happy.
　　　~ Addie

III
All the roses and the champagne and the girls, my God!
　　　~ An American soldier upon liberating Paris

IV
The day after Elie Wiesel died
I tour the store of the second war
to end all wars.

V
In the gift shop
I will not buy my son
the toys of war

VI
I can't conceive
of doing what these men did.
I would be horrible at it. But
I'm thankful they did.

VII
Autocorrect wants to change gift shop
to *girlfriend shop* which is a whole
different kind of shop which I
am not allowed to go into.

Here

The Austrian Consulate stands on the corner
where the first Mardi Gras parade started
for obvious reasons.

Found Hopscotch Court

My wife discovers a hopscotch court on the sidewalk on Magazine Street on our walk back from the museum. Soon, and I mean very soon, she is hopscotching her way across it while other citizens of this space and time are watching, and applauding. The whole thing is filmed thanks to the technology I carry in my pocket. I serve as the narrator, which is really no different from anything else you've read up to this point or, if I'm so lucky, you'll read going on. That's not what's important here though. If you take anything away from this page, let it be the vision of my wife hopscotching on a discovered court on Magazine Street as if she had any other choice.

Melt Everything!

I misread a sign at our hotel that says
Meeting Rooms as *Melting Rooms*.
I think their plans for those rooms
are better than mine.

Perfect

When the woman dressed in the
bald eagle mask wandered into the
middle of the intersection at Chartres
and Frenchman Street to dance
it wasn't clear if she was affiliated
with the horns and drum band
playing on the opposite corner.
But I hope they at least exchanged
cards as another moment that
couldn't be more perfect passed
through our big and easy bones.

Bourbon Street at Night

I
The distinction between streets
and sidewalks is more of a suggestion
in the city where music is in charge.

II
Dancing in the streets.
It's not a metaphor here.

III
The closing time of many
establishments here: until

IV
They always end with Saints.

Jockomo on Bourbon street.
Where else?

Ramos Gin Fizz at the Sazarac

I
The waitress recognizes me.
It's a joyful reunion until I ask
if the table can be cleaned
when she learns to hate me
or maybe it's her job catering
to hypochondriacs issuing
demands. I want every human
to know I'm on her side and
I'm not sure where to go from
here. She's going to hate it when
I pull out my free drink ticket.
This is a losing battle and
I'm the only one who knows
it's raging. My fizzy drink is
coming. This one is for Huey
Long, assassinated in Baton
Rouge. Apparently people
didn't like him either.

II
Addie is just *egging* me on
when she encourages me to
lick the cream off my gin fizz.
You would find this hilarious
If you knew the drink has
an egg in it.

III
It takes a lot of physical effort
to make a gin fizz. You have to
shake it until it's creamy. There's
a story of the bar, at the height of
the drink's popularity, that had to
hire extra people just to shake
the fizzes. You can imagine the
tired bartenders of today
receiving orders for these and
saying *oh shit, I'm tired.*
I'm enjoying the labor sliding
down my throat.

IV
Were getting down to just
cream and fizz when the
horns and drums come on.
I need to hear this like I
need capillaries. We're
fumbling for tip money.
We're permanently doing
this. I'm the sound coming
out of a trombone. The
waitress asks if we're still
doing alright. Can't she tell?
We've never been better.

New Orleans
Day Four

Heavy

The shampoo brand
in our hotel shower
is *Tuscan Soul*
so you can imagine
what I'm going through
right now.

At the Ruby Slipper

*You can't drink all day if you
don't start in the morning.*
              from the Ruby Slipper T-Shirt

I
Double Fisting at
the Ruby Slipper

Mug of coffee in one hand
cup of water in the other

Everything in excess in
the crescent city

II
I found Baton Rouge's red stick
on the floor of the bathroom

at the Canal Street Ruby Slipper.
There's no place like home.

On the Way to the Museum

I
Much of New Orleans is not the French
Quarter, I see, as we streetcar it to the
museum, straight under the 10 Freeway
which crew cuts this nation at the bottom
leaving just one spike on the head of
Lake Pontchartrain.

II
We could have walked to the Museum
but under the right circumstances we
could also walk to Alaska to check in
with Sarah Palin and her troublesome
Russian problem.

New Orleans Museum of Art

I
Bob Dylan, painter
greets us at the New Orleans
Museum of Art

II
*Now let's look at
naked babies and Jesus*
says Addie as we enter
the early Italian section.

III
*Portrait of a Bearded Man
Lorenzo Lotto, 1540*

Sophisticated wolf man and
his fancy blue curtain.

IV
*Meditation of St. Jerome, 1515/20
Benvenuto Tisi, called Il Garofalo*

Gives us all hope we might someday
have dwarf lions as pets.

V
*Death comes to the Banquet Table
Giovanni Martinelli, 1630-40*

Everyone is hoping
he just wants pie.
(Also he's underdressed.)

VI
The chairs in the wall in the Abstraction exhibit
defy all my ideas about where chairs should go.

VII
Penitent Magdalene
Gaspar de Crayer, 17th century

She cries as she cuts her own hair
or threatens to cut it – an act of
penitence for a cloud of black smoke.

VIII
Apollo and the Muses
Maarten van Heemskerck, circa 1555-1560

Naked harp festival or Caligulapalooza.
Angry toddler messes with the piano innards.

IX
Still Life with Fruit, a Lobster and Dead Game
Michiel Simons, 17th Century

Tell it like it is Michiel

X
I feel like I'm walking up stairs for two.
This Bananas Foster Pain Perdu from
breakfast inside me as I make my way
to the third floor to see what it was
like before West African men and women
were put on boats to become
less than human.

XI
Birds, Flowers and Immortals
Yamaguchi Sokeb, 1758-1818

From right to left –

1
Flying saucer brings
this man sausage.

2
Single bird awaits
the arrival of color.

3
River man rides two fish.
Earliest form of transportation.

4
Just nature taking a break
from the immortals.

5
Sleeping man and
his sleeping tiger or
the other way around.

6
Stork or other bird
I can't identify
not being a bird expert.

7
Woman with large square flute
riding fire eyed pig snout devil stagg.
Second oldest form of transportation.

8
Two birds who prefer
trees to fire eyes

9
Man and small pot.
Waiting to see what it will do.

10
One more bird
open mouth
calling for mate
or waiting for food
to fly in.

11
Last man
trying to remember
what it's like to be immortal.

12
Just birds.
No discernible features.
Imagine the silhouettes
of your Japanese youth.

XII
The Cardinal's Friendly Chat
Jehan Georges Vibert, 1880

The pope and a Rabbi
walk into a painting...

XIII
We enter the Inverted Worlds exhibit.
Or do we exit it?

XIV
I found you in New Orleans, Monet.
Your two paintings to Degas' one.
Quite an achievement since he
lived here for a time.

XV
A button says "Tap to start."
My God an hour into this museum
and I haven't even started yet.

XVI
Two hooks where a panting should be.
No sign explaining *installation in progress*.
I suspect theft or I'm missing the artistry
of hooks.

XVII
I should have asked before I dropped
is something I should have said for
reasons you don't need to know about.

XVIII
We take a selfie in the gold cabin.
I can't possibly be the first person
To use the word selfie in a poem.

XIX
The Park of Saint-Cloud
Hubert Robert, circa 1760

is the last painting we look at
at the New Orleans Museum of Art
before we head out into the park
where clouds and saints wait
to shield us from the elements
of July on the bayou.

XX
Someone has left the water running in the bathroom.
I suspect it wasn't on purpose. We're so used to
faucets and things that activate and turn off automatically
when we wave our hands. One can imagine physically
turning off a faucet is what cavemen used to do.

XXI
When seeing Pietro Consagra's sculpture
Conversation with the Moon Addie wonders
what that conversation would consist of. She
starts with a cute "hello" but then loses interest
and walks off to the blue dog sculpture.

XXII
The order taker at the museum cafe
tells us to take a seat and the food will
find us. Now he has me all concerned
about sentient food.

XXIII
1776 t-shirt and
red white and blue
American flag underwear.
There is no-one more
patriotic than me on this
fourth of July in the
art museum.

Bam

I want to dine at all the fine restaurants in New Orleans and ask the waiters halfway through the meal if they have any of Emeril's Cajun seasoning. *I Just want to bam it up a bit.* Have they heard of Emeril? Addie crawls under the table when I tell her this.

Waiting for Fireworks on the Mississippi

I'm losing count of how many times we've waited by some body of water for the sky to go up in flames. Year after year in city after city. Remember the ones on July 12th in the city that behaved a little differently from the rest? Here's to a hundred more years of the sky lightning up our evenings. These rivers flow through our lives together like a Mark Twain.

Amuse Bouche

The pre-fireworks in Algiers
which is not another country
but a community across the river
home grown or stand bought
hardly an inch or two over their
buildings. They wet our appetite
for the America that is coming.

Waiting for a Seat

I
Seats at the carousel in the Carousel Bar
at Hotel Monteleone are rare like coming
late to the goldfish party.

(And at this point I'm wondering what I
really meant after discovering "goldfish party"
in this text and assuming autocorrect has
had its way with me.)

I want to sit at a tiger or a lion but
I'll settle for anything with a cushion.
and one for my lovely wife too.

II
Of course we have to wait for a seat
at the carousel because who doesn't
want to slowly revolve while alcohol
is going inside you. They should throw
in a couple of terrifying clowns to
complete the experience.

Vieux Carré

The Vieux Carré has the strength of
a hundred men. We missed Royal street

on the way here and had to Bourbon Street.
You can make verbs out of anything.

I'm sitting on a lion and Addie has, our best
guess is, a gibbon. Spellcheck has

no idea what to do with the name of this
drink. I have no idea how many sips

it'll be before this circular motion spills
me out the door or window or into the

hotel proper. The fireworks are a memory
that will only become more distant.

Like the ones from last year which we
didn't even see because we were

on another continent. I forget how
many continents there are. Is it

seven or did one get demoted like
Pluto? The man next to me wants food

but the kitchen has been closed since
before the sky exploded. My advice

to him and to anyone listening -
always have dinner before ten p.m.

Addie wants to give him a peanut
butter packet. I want to apologize

to the man I said *happy new year* to.
I correct and say *Independence Day* and

he says *yeah well do that one today.*
Today is almost yesterday. My bed

is a woozy few blocks away. My
pillow turned down. It's meeting

with my head
inevitable.

Seated at the Carousel

I
When two seats open up next to me
on the carousel, and two new people
sit down. I want to tell them "welcome
To captain Ricky's Revolving World
Of wonder." Addie is talking to the person
next to her so she doesn't even know
to prevent me from doing this.

II
Cities are amazing and so
far apart. The woman next to us
is from Chicago where they also
have roads and buildings and
restaurants. Like here, though,
the two never touch. All of this
could be the Vieux Carré talking.

III
Addie tells me not to move while
she conducts separate business
apart from the carousel. But you
will move she acknowledges
because of the nature of
operating carousels.

IV
Is this carousel moving faster
or am I already back in Los Angeles?

New Orleans Day Five

I Can Dress Myself

We're heading to a swamp today
so I ready my outfit which consists
of alligator paint and leaves all of
which is quickly vetoed by Addie.

(Actually she's having breakfast
downstairs so I just assume she
would veto this. [I'm learning people!])

Driving to the Swamp

I
Ronnie from Pearl River Eco Tours
picks us up in the shuttle bus to
take us to the swamp. And we
were never heard from again.

II
When we get on the bus
I want to announce to the
passengers already on board:
Hello fellow swamp people!
But Addie has already pre-vetoed
any direct interaction with
other people.

III
I wore a button-down short-sleeved
shirt to the swamp. I want the alligators
to know I made an effort.

IV
I hope they have trash cans in
the bayou as I just can't take
this empty coffee cup anymore.

V
Once you get out of
New Orleans, you're no longer
in New Orleans.

VI
We're on the 10 Freeway again
heading straight towards Florida.
I hope we stop before we get that far.

VII
When I check in at Lake Pontchartrain
Foursquare tells mean it's my first lake.
Oh sweet Foursquare, I thought you
knew me better than that.

VIII
I am committed to declining any offer
to put my head inside an alligator.

IX
We pass a store called *Bam!*
where I believe you can purchase
Emeril Lagasse fingers.

In the Swamp

I
On the inside of the boat it says
"Keep hand and 'eet' inside boat."
Alligator already got to that one.

II
We learn the difference between
real alligators and tour alligators.

III
We pass through a fishing village
the sign says to go *Dead Slow*.

IV
Our guide has been doing these tours
for fifteen years so I assume he knows
the way back.

(Queue the *Deliverance* theme song...)

V
I see Tom Sawyer and Huckleberry Finn
bass fishing like they've been doing since
before they called him Mark Twain.

VI
A swamp is a forest that is under water.

VII
We back away from the descendant
of a pig the Spanish brought. No one
considered marshmallows at the time
but two are left floating in the water
The pig, a recent mother, gets smaller
as our boat goes. It's unlikely I'll
see her again.

VIII
Addie agrees the swamp is beautiful
but rebutes my declaration that we
should move here.

IX
Two different boat drivers we pass
declare our driver their grandson.
One tells us *pretty* skips a generation.

X
I see more than one human-made
bottle floating in the river. People
are the worst.

XI
I'm reminded so much
of the world is not
paved over.

XII
The *alligators in the swamp* experience
Was much better than the *alligator
in the other alligators mouth* in the
New York alligator pit experience.

After the Swamp

I
Back at the base waiting on another tour.
No one sees their boat, but there are some
fat looking alligators back there.

II
Back on our bus with my photos and
poetry intact. Glad I didn't pre-throw
my phone into the swamp.

III
Be nice or leave
a sign in the tour shack says.
Well, I was nice, but we're leaving
anyway. The tour is over.

When I Die

When I die
have a jazz funeral.
Second line it. Make it funny.
Guys dressed as Groucho
rainbow suspenders
comic arrows through their heads.

When I die
bury me in an above ground cemetery.
Put up a ladder so people can climb
up and see as far as they can see.

When I die
turn my house into a museum.
Let people open the cabinets and
see how I hid the curios from my travels.
Let the smaller ones try on my outfits.
Make cat petting a free add on experience.
Actually make that mandatory.

When I die
take my wife in your arms.
Don't let her feel alone.

haiku

My favorite place in
the world is anywhere horns
and drums are playing.

Killer PoBoys

On the map, the restaurant Killer PoBoys and the Death Museum are in the same spot which doesn't bode well for the restaurant's sandwiches.

Bridges Cross Lake Pontchartrain

Over salt water that
the alligators we just saw
could never ingest.

Humanity conquers
the lake, as far as the
eyes can see..

Adam and Eve

We walk by *The Rib Room*.
I've still got mostly a full set
so we don't stop in.

Mardy Gras

If they spell *Mardi Gras* wrong on their sign that's not where you should buy your Mardi Gras supplies.

At The Jazz Exhibit

I
At the free concert at the Jazz museum
at the Old US Mint. The bandleader asks
his band if F is good for everyone before
launching into *Careless Love*. Such a carefree
question to ask before this carefree song.

II
Soon there will be a new Jazz Museum
It's a gift to the world.

III
*We're right here with the colored folk and
the Puerto Ricans and Italians and the
Hebrew cats, what the hell do I care about
living in a 'fashionable neighborhood'?"*
 - Louis Armstrong on living in Queens

A Quote

That wallet's too hard to get out of my fish
Addie says for obvious reasons.

They Go Hand in Paw

It's gotten to the point when
I walk into a used bookstore
or even an independent seller
of new books, I expect there to
be at least one cat, waiting to
be petted. Not that it will acknowledge
any enjoyment of this. But it won't
protest either. So when I walk in to
Librairie Book Shop on Chartres street
and they don't seem to have a cat
I just assume it's on its break, rather
than declare the whole bookshop
to be illegitimate.

Pimm's Cup

This drink is delicious but it's so well mixed
I'm not sure it's working yet. We're waiting for
it to take hold. Napoleon almost lived in this
room but he died before he was rescued.
A pirate was involved. The mayor lived here
but doesn't still live here. The classical music
is the first we've heard in this city of music
and perhaps the first evidence of anything
refined, unless you count the restaurant
from last night which was more serious
than anything. I don't think this room has
been painted since 1797. I think I just tasted
gin – the master of disguises of liqueurs.
A couple we recognize from the museum today
sits nearby. I ask Addie if we are following them.
This is the first evidence the Pimm's is working.
No one wants to have a beverage repaired.
Because of brass and drums we will not have
dinner for hours. I will float on this drink to the
edge of the French Quarter. That is my Waterloo.
The two Louis – Prima and Armstrong.
They'll take care of this.

This Just in From Addie Who Still Refuses to Write Her Own Book

As we passed by a restaurant sign
that says *Déjà Vu Bar and Grill,* Addie says
*I just wish there was another one of these signs
about a block away.*

Maple Leaf Bar

It's a Tuesday night
Time for a *Rebirth*
A brass band
Drums and horns
Other side of town
Six microphones
Full house
Cash only
Gonna second line
all night, or
as much as
my old bones
can stand
Maybe this
is my Jazz
Funeral
I want to go
right now

Career

If I only knew how
to play the trumpet.
I could pack a room.
I wouldn't have to
write all this poetry.

Well Placed Audience Member

Treme shirt
Saint in his hat
He belongs here.

Artistic Driving

When I get home I want to be an Uber driver like all the ones we've met here, and a poet for hire like the ones on Frenchman Street. Except to save time I'm going to combine them and be an Uber Poet for hire. Addie doesn't think that sounds safe.

New Orleans Day Six

Good Morning New Orleans

Your last night is still ringing
in my ear. It is cold inside your
buildings, and burning water
outside your doors.
Our last day is
a cup of coffee away.

In Mister Gregory's Cafe

I
The barista at Mister Gregory's
tells Addie he has flamingo
everything. Our voodoo tour
is about to begin so I can't
spend too much time listing
everything I can think of
to see if he has THAT in
flamingo form.

II
The book *New Orleans for Free*
costs five dollars. That's how they
get you.

On the Voodoo Tour

I
A woman brings her
baby on the Voodoo tour
for early indoctrination.

II
One party on the tour has
not arrived, and they never do.

III
Our tour guide, Melissa, lives in the Treme
which is all the street cred. she needs.

IV
Secret Voodoo worshippers
disguised as Catholics
like Jews secretly lighting
candles in their basements
in 1492.

V
They linked their Voodoo Gods
to Catholic Saints to keep
up appearances in the days
of the *Code Noir*.

VI
The guide talks so loud and so fast.
It must be a Voodoo incantation that
keeps her from exploding.

VII
There are many similarities
between Judaism and Voodoo.
I'm going to combine the two
and call it Jew Joo.

VIII
The *Loa* are very particular
about who they ride.
The *Ghede* will ride
almost anyone.

IX
Marie Laveau was
the Voodoo Moses

X
Car horns sound like trumpets.
Everyone's involved with the second line.

XI
Marie Laveau's daughter, Marie Laveau,
took over the family business and
made it seem like Marie never aged
or died.

XII
We pass by the *Biscuit Palace*.
Yes, if any food deserved a palace
it's biscuits.

XIII
The caucasian, preppy dressed man
tapping on his cell phone, blocking
the Marie Laveau shrine is actually
a Voodoo practitioner who is
purposefully stationed where he is.
You can't judge a Voodoo queen
by his cover.

XIV
There is a *Linksys* router
inside *Voodoo Authentica*.
It is an authentic wireless router.
We use the tools of our day.

XV
Addie buys some gris-gris
I think that's great great.

You Get What You Pay For

One store on Royal Street
is selling tutus at fifty percent off.
But you only get a tu.

Modification

Addie wants her PoBoy without bread. She's not sure whether to ask for it without the *Po* or without the *Boy*.

Marital Privilege

Addie asks if I want to smell her gris-gris.
This is not a metaphor.

At Killer PoBoys

We got here just in time
as the line grows behind us
at the PoBoy shop. Then she
leans in and her lips, soft
like hotel pillows, touch mine
at exactly the right time.

At the Pharmacy Museum

*Why should a man die who
grows sage in his garden?*

I
There's an exhibit
of old spectacles.
It is spectacleular.
Thank you.

II
Condoms were illegal
because they were thought
to be too pornographic.

III
Have you heard of the miasma?
The theory that all diseases were
caused by bad air? The cure was
to purge all air and water. By the
time 1880 came around, after so
much purging, bacteria took over
as the cause of bad things.

IV
People wanted to be seen
consuming precious metal
so they opted for gold and
silver coated pills which would
pass right through them
rendering them reusable
and inheritable.

V
Curved table legs,
the guide tells us, were *the*
other side of the aphrodisiac
spectrum from Spanish fly.
What furniture turns you on?

VI
Heroine and red wine
the guide tells us
was marketed as
'Mothers Quietness.'

VII
Mind your own beeswax
referred to the wax makeup
people would apply for beauty
that would then melt off their faces.
Also losing face.

VIII
The Essence of Bend Over
sold out a long time ago so
no one is sure what it did.

At The New Orleans Collection Museum

I
We're about to do our last attraction.
Are you feeling melancholy about this?
I am.

II
Men like maps
we're told in the museum.
I like maps I tell her.
Men like maps she says
even more confidently.

III
So many opportunities to
use my fancy voice in this old
house turned museum.
This is where we'll dine tonight...
This is where I'll take my cocktails tonight...
I won't shut up about it.

The Old Absinthe Inn

Pernod Absinthe
poured over sugar

sitting on a slotted spoon
set on fire

corner of Bourbon and
another street.

A writer nearby
Hemingway on

his counter
plus a pen

and paper
salutes our

absinthe
choice.

My Absinthe choice...
The old fountain is here

with lead pipes –
Wormwood blamed

for the sins of
tainted water.

I'm in a cloud.

At one bar you can get

a *Wet Pussy* or a *Blowjob*.
These are beverages people.
Calm your kinky asses down.

Solution

You could house every American inside all the cheeks of every horn blower.

At NOLA Restaurant

They clear the crumbs away
so we are not eating like cave-people
tonight.

Chaz at DBA

Harmonica
guitar
washboard
A trio
Like the Violent Femmes
Only more about fishing
One drink minimum
Tip the band
Drinks count as tips
Mississippi
Blue

Another Ramos Gin Fizz

I could have any drink in the world
but nostalgia brings me back to this one.
My memory three days old. Strong
and old.

We walk down Bourbon Street and
a swingers parade has broken out.
You have to be invited to
go to the after party.

It is a Wednesday, so naturally
the party on this street is in full swing.
Beads rain out of the sky. Barriers
don't block the intersections but

cars wouldn't dare go down it.
Every restaurant and strip club
and music salon personally
invites us in. We're just here

for the memories and they stop at
Canal Street where there never was
a canal. Here at the house of
our libations the bartenders grow

strong muscles performing their
gin fizzes. One is being shaken for me.
It will travel to our table on an animal
that is somewhere between

a horse and a mule. Bred this way
to tolerate these late hours. Here it comes.
Here it is. Tomorrow I'll be in states that
don't understand the word *parish*.

I only got it this week. You can
learn anything if someone tells
it to you. Oh, the things I will tell
people when I cross the mountains

where the air has no water. Where my cats
will come out from under the bed and say
where have you been? Don't do that again.
But I will.

Leaving New Orleans Which One Should Never Do

Leaving New Orleans

Our driver doesn't tell us about the
plants and trees we see on the road
like the one in to town did.

He knows leaving New Orleans
is like a death with no parade and he
doesn't want to exacerbate our condition.

This Ten Freeway could take us all the
way home, or at least to the Four-Oh-Five,
but we'll only get as far as the

Louis Armstrong International Airport
where one last beignet is waiting for us
just this side of security.

They keep it on the New Orleans side of
security because they know once we taste it,
we'll change our minds,

head back into the city
that bleeds music and
not think about leaving.

Catch 22

You can't take water through airport security but the human body is sixty to sixty-five percent water. No one say anything or they'll cancel airline travel.

Like Back in the Cave-Day

Even though we are *TSA Pre-Check*
I have to take my laptop out of my bag.
I imagine this is how cavemen used to
get through airport security.

Flying Like Cave-People

On the plane, in the front row, it looks like they didn't clean the crumbs off the seat before we boarded. I suspect this is how cavemen originally travelled First Class.

Everywhere

Everything I know about North Carolina
will be contained in the Charlotte airport.

I'm looking forward to sampling their
lunchtime cuisine. I remind Addie she

has been to Charlotte. It's one of the
places we haven't yet shared. As the

years turn to more years, fewer places
have hosted just one set of our feet.

Someday the whole world will have
put its air inside us.

Flight Number Five

We lift off Louisiana ground.
This is really happening.

Clouds try to steal my last
view of the city. But they can't.

I can see the art museum and
it's sculpture garden. The Super-

dome, repaired after a decade
old memory of high winds and

refugees. There's the Mississippi.
We'll fly over her one more time

in a couple days. The clouds
win. Or maybe it's the growing

distance. Bridges over Lake
Pontchartrain. I've been there.

Addie tells me this city
makes me weep.

Did I already say that?
It's worth saying again.

Lehigh Valley

I'm in Bethlehem, Pennsylvania

I'm not the first one to make a pilgrimage
here. Some came to find their savior.
I'm here for brunch. You can't get
a quiche east of MacArthur Boulevard
to save your soul. I'm alone. Just for
the afternoon. It's the first time
I've spent any minutes without
Addie's breath a breath away since
we left the homeland. I prefer the
other moments, but I'll take the quiet
for what it's worth. The restaurant is
closed when I pull up. There's no
salvation for this hungry boy.

I Drive By

I
I drive by *Nuts Ice Cream*.
They'll make ice cream
out of anything.

II
I drive by a sign that says
Lehigh Valley Mental Health Hospital
on a large field of grass with no buildings.
When I finally lose it I want you to
put me here. Let the grass grow tall.
Let it cover everything
but the sign.

Blue Sky

I
The waitress says I can sit wherever
I want. I ask if I can sit at the booth
meant for a hundred people. She says
she never should have opened her mouth.
How would she eat then, I wonder,
even working here in a cafe?

II
I'm sitting in the Blue Sky Cafe
in *Courtney's Booth*.
She's not here.
But her plaque is.

III
Your vitamin is on the kitchen counter
Addie told me. The problem is the
kitchen counter is ten miles from
the restaurant I am sitting in. I
believe it's still there though.

Flight Number Six

Nothing worth mentioning happens on flight number six.

Flight Number Seven

This begins and ends on an airplane. Even the Pennsylvania sky has a hard time with this ending. It pours tears on our car. Soon America will go by our coach class windows. Mountains and cities we have yet to visit. Rivers we have yet to cross or stand next to. The Mississippi is in our future. Maybe six hours away. I'll drop this poem from the plane. Don't ask how. Let it ride the air down to the water. Float on a frog down to Louisiana. Let someone see it from the Steamboat Natchez. Let it float to the shore where another visitor will imagine its origin. I'm already over the desert. The expanse of Los Angeles is all anyone can see. We descend. It swallows us. Who knows the next place that will steal our hearts. Scotland, the Carolinas. The whole world wants me to write about it. Or maybe it's me. Until next year. My finger are ready.

Postscript

At LAX
an escalator
almost eats
Addie.

*That's how
I lost my
first wife* I
tell Jude.

Her shoelace
the only
casualty.
It's not a
myth people!

About The Author

The author making friends in New Orleans

Two-time Pushcart Prize nominee Rick Lupert has been involved in the Los Angeles poetry community since 1990. He was awarded the Beyond Baroque Distinguished Service Award in 2014 for service to the Los Angeles poetry community. He served for two years as a co-director of the non-profit literary organization Valley Contemporary Poets. His poetry has appeared in numerous magazines and literary journals, including *The Los Angeles Times, Rattle, Chiron Review, Red Fez, Zuzu's Petals, Stirring, The Bicycle Review, Caffeine Magazine, Blue Satellite* and others. He edited the anthologies *Ekphrastia Gone Wild - Poems Inspired by Art, A Poet's Haggadah: Passover through the Eyes of Poets*, and *The Night Goes on All Night - Noir Inspired Poetry*, and is the author of nineteen other books: *Romancing the Blarney Stone, Professor Clown on Parade, Making Love to the 50 Ft. Woman, The Gettysburg Undress* (Rothco Press), *Nothing in New England is New, Death of a Mauve Bat, Sinzibuckwud!, We Put Things In Our Mouths, Paris: It's The Cheese, I Am My Own Orange County, Mowing Fargo, I'm a Jew. Are You?, Feeding Holy Cats, Stolen Mummies, I'd Like to Bake Your Goods, A Man With No Teeth Serves Us Breakfast* (Ain't Got No Press), *Lizard King of the Laundromat, Brendan Constantine is My Kind of Town* (Inevitable Press) and *Up Liberty's Skirt* (Cassowary Press), and the spoken word album "Rick Lupert Live and Dead" (Ain't Got No Press). He hosted the long running Cobalt Café reading series in Canoga Park for almost twenty-one years and has read his poetry all over the world.

Rick created and maintains Poetry Super Highway, an online resource and publication for poets (PoetrySuperHighway.com), Haikuniverse, a daily online small poem publication (Haikuniverse.com), and writes and occasionally draws the daily web comic Cat and Banana with Brendan Constantine. (facebook.com/catandbanana) He also writes the weekly Jewish poetry blog "From the Lupertverse" for JewishJournal.com

Currently Rick works as a music teacher at synagogues in Southern California and as a graphic and web designer for anyone who would like to help pay his mortgage.

Rick's Other Books and Recordings

Romancing the Blarney Stone
Rothco Press ~ December, 2016

Professor Clown on Parade
Rothco Press ~ December, 2016

Rick Lupert Live and Dead (Album)
Ain't Got No Press ~ March, 2016

Making Love to the 50 Ft. Woman
Rothco Press ~ May, 2015

The Gettysburg Undress
Rothco Press ~ May, 2014

Ekphrastia Gone Wild (edited by)
Ain't Got No Press ~ July, 2013

Nothing in New England is New
Ain't Got No Press ~ March, 2013

Death of a Mauve Bat
Ain't Got No Press ~ January, 2012

The Night Goes On All Night
Noir Inspired Poetry (edited by)
Ain't Got No Press ~ November, 2011

Sinzibuckwud!
Ain't Got No Press ~ January, 2011

We Put Things In Our Mouths
Ain't Got No Press ~ January, 2010

A Poet's Haggadah (edited by)
Ain't Got No Press ~ April, 2008

A Man With No Teeth
Serves Us Breakfast
Ain't Got No Press ~ May, 2007

I'd Like to Bake Your Goods
Ain't Got No Press ~ January, 2006

Stolen Mummies
Ain't Got No Press ~ February, 2003

Brendan Constantine is My Kind of Town
Inevitable Press ~ September, 2001

Up Liberty's Skirt
Cassowary Press ~ March, 2001

Feeding Holy Cats
Cassowary Press ~ May, 2000

I'm a Jew, Are You?
Cassowary Press ~ May, 2000

Mowing Fargo
Sacred Beverage Press ~ December, 1998

Lizard King of the Laundromat
The Inevitable Press ~ February, 1998

I Am My Own Orange County
Ain't Got No Press ~ May, 1997

Paris: It's The Cheese
Ain't Got No Press ~ May, 1996

For more information:
http://PoetrySuperHighway.com/

www.ingramcontent.com/pod-product-compliance
Lightning Source LLC
Chambersburg PA
CBHW071729080526
44588CB00013B/1957